Yannis Ritsos (1909–1990)  family, though his childhood fortune was lost to gambling and political vicissitude, his father and, later, his sister were declared insane and confined to asylums; his mother and brother died of TB within months of each other; Ritsos himself fell victim to the disease and spent years in sanatoria.

Ritsos's commitment to Marxism caused his work to be banned, and the poet to be imprisoned or exiled, by successive right-wing regimes. He nonetheless continued to write and published in excess of 100 books. Ritsos is widely considered to be among the great Greek poets of the twentieth century. He was several times nominated for the Nobel Prize.

David Harsent has published nine volumes of poetry: *Legion* won the Forward Prize for Best Collection; his most recent collection, *Night,* won the Griffin International Poetry Prize. Harsent has collaborated with composers on commissions performed at major venues, including the Royal Opera House, the Royal Albert Hall (Proms), the Edinburgh International Festival, the Aldeburgh Festival and Carnegie Hall.

David Harsent

In Secret

Versions of Yannis Ritsos

ENITHARMON PRESS

First published in 2012
by Enitharmon Press
26B Caversham Road
London NW5 2DU

www.enitharmon.co.uk

Distributed in the UK by
Central Books
99 Wallis Road
London E9 5LN

ISBN: 978-1-907587-21-4

Enitharmon Press gratefully acknowledges the financial support of
Arts Council England through Grants for the Arts.

British Library Cataloguing-in-Publication Data.
A catalogue record for this book is available
from the British Library.

Designed in Albertina by Libanus Press
and printed in England by
Antony Rowe Ltd

The frontispiece reproduces a drawing by Yannis Ritsos, by kind permission of Ery Ritsou.

for Ciaran Carson

ACKNOWLEDGEMENTS

Thanks to the editors of the following journals where some of the poems in this book first appeared: *Blinking Eye; Great River Review* (USA); *London Review of Books; Magma; Modern Poetry in Translation; Poetry* (USA); *Poetry Review;* the Royal Opera House programme for *The Minotaur* (libretto: David Harsent; music: Harrison Birtwistle); *The Spectator; Times Literary Supplement; The Yellow Nib.*

A shorter version of the Afterword first appeared in *Great River Review*. I am much indebted to Alice Kavounas and Fotini Dimou for supplying me with literal translations of a number of the poems and to Ery Ritsou for authorising this collection.

D. H.

CONTENTS

A BREAK IN ROUTINE

They came to the door and read names from a list.
If you heard your name you had to get ready fast:
a busted suitcase, a bundle you might carry
over your shoulder, perhaps; forget the rest.
With each new departure, the place seemed to shrink.

Finally, those who were left agreed to bunk
in a single room, which no one thought odd.
They found an old alarm clock
and placed it just here, in the hearth,
a little household god,
and made a rota for who would wind it and set it
to ring at six-thirty, in time for their needle-bath.

Once, it went off at midnight, whereat they woke
and sluiced themselves under the moon, then sat
in a circle round the clock
to smoke the last of their cigarettes.

1972

Each night, gunfire. Come dawn, a sudden silence.
Blank walls, floors scrubbed clean, chairs arranged just so.

Think of a door, and beyond it a door,
and another door beyond that, the spaces between
crammed with the kind of cotton-waste they use
to fill the mouths of the starving or the dead.

Our heroes are small men, pasty-faced and fat.

THE ACCUSED

Just as he locked the door, as he pocketed the key,
as he glanced over his shoulder, they arrested him.
They tortured him until they tired of it.
                                          'Look,' they said,
'the key is your key, the house is your house,
we accept that now; but why did you put the key
in your pocket as if to hide it from us?'

They let him go, but his name is still on a list.

MIDNIGHT

The arcade was in darkness. She was dressed in black.
Her footsteps on the stairs were feather-light.
'Halt!' they shouted, 'Halt!' Her violin was hidden
beneath her smock. She gripped it between her knees
and turned to them, hands raised, and smiling, smiling.

WAITING FOR DAYBREAK

Night comes slowly here. No one sleeps. We wait
for the hammer-blows of the sun on tin roofs,
on our heads, on our hearts; and wait for that to displace
the sound of gunfire from somewhere out in the darkness.

WOMEN

Our women are distant, their sheets smell of goodnight.
They put bread on the table as a token of themselves.
It's then that we finally see we were at fault; we jump up saying,
'Look, you've done too much, take it easy, I'll light the lamp.'

She turns away with the striking of the match,
walking towards the kitchen, her face in shadow, her back
bent under the weight of so many dead –
those you both loved, those she loved, those
you alone loved . . . yes . . . and your death also.

Listen: the bare boards creaking where she goes.
Listen: the dishes weeping in the dishrack.
Listen: the train taking soldiers to the front.

THE WRITING TABLE

Remember when you wrote a poem a day
at this old table? Now it's full of worm-holes,
of bullet-holes. The night-wind plays it like a flute.

Sometimes, just before dawn, Urania descends.
She sets her white gloves down on that same table,
her white handbag, her starry bangles,
and lies beside you while you sleep. Or else pretend to sleep.

THE VISITOR

He reached the house. He lifted his hand to knock.
But then . . . suppose they answered, suppose a face
appeared at an upstairs window, suppose
someone put out the garbage: dog-ends,
dead flowers, the letter he'd left two days before.

Night came on. The place stayed dark,
not even a light on the landing. Even so,
he could see, in the hall, a litter of cola cans,
spent cartridges, his death-mask slightly foxed.

THE TRIAL

A day like any other at first; but here come the mourners,
scuffing their feet, heads down, as if bone-weary.
They are wearing coats that no longer quite fit; in the pockets,
pieces of funeral-bread too dry to eat.
When they think no one's looking they let the fragments fall.
The dead man's mother, wrapped in her black, collects the crumbs –
evidence for when the survivors come to trial.

THE BOX

We measured up, we threw lime over the dead.
As we got aboard, a sickle moon broke through.
Four of us: one carried the iron-bound box on his lap
and huddled over it like a man warming himself
at his fireside. There was smoke low on the water.

IN SECRET

They were calling across the water, calling a name.
Once he was sure it was his he ran and hid.
An ocean-going liner slipped out of the harbour
all lights blazing, on the upper-deck a woman
wearing a picture hat. It blocked his view
of the dark tower, the moon, the waiting scaffold.

ON COLOUR

Red mountain. Green sea. Yellow sky.
And the earth is blue.

A bird. A leaf.
And perched between them, death.

RITUAL

You could hear the drumbeat for miles.
They slaughtered a dove,

a chicken, a goat, and smeared the blood
on their faces and necks.

One of them turned away; when he turned back,
blood was dripping from his cock and balls.

They drew on the floor with chalk – serpents and arrows,
bent to their task, as if they couldn't see

those three young girls in the corner, veiled in white;
as if they couldn't hear those tiny cries.

THE BELL

Our lamp still burns at daybreak, ochre with a touch of blue.
A smell of gas from the stove, the smell of coffee,
and a musty smell that might be the smell of age.
Playing-cards litter the table; the ashtrays are full.

Men and women. Gardens and books. They come and go.
And that tinny tinkle you heard
just before dawn wasn't the mail arriving.
It was the old bell-wether leading lambs to the slaughter.

THE CRANE DANCE

The clew paying out through his fingers, a deftness
that would bring him back to her, its softness the softness
of skin, as if drawn from herself directly, the faint
labial smell, guiding him up and out, as some dampness
on the air might lead a stone-blind man to the light.

Asterios dead for sure, his crumpled horn, his muzzle
thick with blood . . . So at Delos they stopped,
Theseus and the young Athenians, and stepped
up to the altar of horns to dance a puzzle-
dance, its moves unreadable except to those who'd walked
the blank meanders of the labyrinth.
And this was midday: a fierce sun, the blaze
of their nakedness, the glitter of repetitions, a dazzle
rising off the sea, the scents of pine and hyacinth . . .

Well, things change: new passions, new threats, new fears.
New consequences, too. Nowadays, we don't think much
about Theseus, the Minotaur, Ariadne on the beach
at Naxos, staring out at the coming years.
But people still dance that dance: just common folk,
those criss-cross steps that no one had to teach,
at weddings and wakes, in bars or parks,
as if hope and heart could meet, as if they might
even now, somehow, dance themselves out of the dark.

THE VIEW

The trees, the well, the flower-beds, the statues,
the benches where we sat, now wet with rain...

As he showed us the view from the window
there was still a vague smile in his eyes

until the garden-boy arrived, bare-chested,
hefting a sack of seed. That's when

he slammed the shutters and showed us, instead,
the place where that picture used to hang

of two women, naked, a guard, a gallows-tree.

THE WOUND

No one heard the shot, but he clapped a hand to his chest
to staunch the blood. A long moment later
he took out his wallet. He paid the bill and left.

He'd been gone a minute, no more, when his coffee cup
cracked from top to bottom. We all heard that.

HERE IS THE NEWS

Red-tops, revolts, denials, discoveries, deaths,
dust and darkness and sweat

The all-night
pharmacy, a ladder climbing to meet—

Usury, murder, pi-dogs, whores,
prisons, a creeping sea-fret, muggings,
beggars, the blind, blind beggars, bad odour, bad laws

A guitar,
the tree, the streetlamp, the hangings

In the space
between two tall chimneys, a single star

Thank you

The key to my door is in the usual place

from AGAMEMNON

The city was still smouldering end to end. We buried the dead,
then, at twilight, went down to the beach and set tables
for the victory feast. When Helen lifted her glass, the bracelets
rattled on her wrist. 'Listen to that,' she said, 'I must be dead.'

At once a piercing white light shone out from her mouth
and all within its range was marble and bone. Voices died.
Hands locked in a gesture. Our ships were white, the sea was white, a white
gull pitched out of the sky and landed on the table by the wine jugs.

She dipped her finger in its blood and drew a circle on the cloth – the sum
of nothing, the sum of everything – then ripped a tuft of feathers
from its breast and cast them into the wind: they caught in our hair.
That omen we could ignore, but not the taste of whiteness, that perfect circle.

THE DEAD HOUSE

We live alone, my sister and I. We are the youngest,
now grown old. We are the youngest, the rest are dead.
We can't cope with the house. We can't cope with each other.
We can't sell up because our dead live here with us.
They belong to the place; they've settled in
behind curtains, under tables, in the backs of mirrors.
I can see one now caught in the shadow-saltire
cast by my sister's knitting-needles, and smiling shyly.

All the old furniture is locked away downstairs:
heavy-legged tables and chairs, sheets and blankets,
quilts of silk, silver salvers, the antique crystal,
tablecloths, monogrammed napkins, the hundred-piece
dinner service, riding habits and whips,
the piano, guitars and accordions, flutes and drums,
chandeliers, the gilt-framed dining-room mirrors,
dolls and a rocking horse, gewgaws and trinkets,
the long white dresses our mother liked to wear,
our father's uniform, his boots and spurs.

Our own clothes hang beside the clothes of the dead.

We have nailed the doors shut on all this. We keep two rooms
on the upper floor, facing west; our corridor leads
to the back-stair – now and then we walk in the garden at night.
The empty house breeds echoes: mouse-run, bat-flight,
spiders building webs in the cellar, the creep of rust in a knife-blade.

We are not much more than shadow, a hint, a trace,
as when you cut flowers for the sick-room and a smudge
of pollen stains your fingers, or dust from the road outside
sifts in through the lattice, and the flowers carry
a dewdrop caught in gossamer, barely there.

Everything has left us, or we have left everything.

Once it was noise and light, voices and music, soldiers home
from the front. Yes, I remember that – big peasants' hands,
lice in their underwear, hard-mouthed as if they had kissed
the faces of dead comrades once too often. They would sing
in the kitchen at night. My sister and I would listen
behind the door. The kitchen was out of bounds: its smells
of blood and milk, the whisper of knives, the ribs and stumps.
Sometimes we'd find a spillage of salt,
or a cockerel's head on the path that led to the trash.

Kitchen-girls at the cauldrons conjured a wraith
from the steam: a woman in white, one of the slaughtered.
If someone opened the door for just a moment
she would sidle out and stand there looking lost.
The soldiers sang and drank; they got the girls
up on the table and lifted their skirts. I like to think
those children came to be born
in a house of fewer shadows, a house of lockless doors.

The girls knew the soldiers' song: of victory, of banners and flags,
of the General marching back at the head of his troops,
of the wound he bore on his brow, a sleepless eye
out of which stared Death, so Death and the General could see
into the souls of men, and name their sin.

'Let him come,' our mother said. 'Let him come home'.

I remember . . . An owl flew across the forecourt, unlucky in daylight.
Its shadow's still there on the lintel above the gate.
The kitchen-girls ran inside. Our mother filled a bath
with scalding water and lay there; later, she went to her room
and put on her make-up: red lips, deep red. The sun
was setting fast and all the church bells rang.

Everything has left us, or we have left everything.

We got some village women in to cook and clean.
They didn't last. They said the marble floor was sweating blood.
The locals used to cross themselves and spit
as they passed the house. Now no one comes by.
The road outside is weeds, wildflowers and thorn.

Some nights I see those long white dresses in the orchard,
lit by moonlight, lifted by the wind,
as if they were walking or dancing…though, of course,
I see nothing, remember nothing, nor hear the music
that would play all night and you'd wake, for no reason, at dawn
the morning air thick with birdsong, no space for hope
or remorse, and time locked-off by the strangeness of it all.

Can you feel that cut in the air – the edge of Autumn?
Soon we'll close the windows against the chill
and light fires in the grates. We'll gather logs from the orchard
and from the woods beyond but, of course, if that falls short
there's plenty to burn: doors, beds, roof-beams, sideboards, shutters,
floorboards, tables and chairs, pictures and books,
all and everything from the downstairs rooms.

We will sit here until the fires burn out, until the ash
grows cold, until the house is held in boundless night.

THE ACROBAT

He walked on his hands, so perfectly upside-down
that he seemed to make past present, present past.

Then the floor opened and swallowed him.
We looked at each other: who would ever believe us?

A moment later, the doorbell rang.
There he stood, with a basket of oranges.

ALMOST

It was just luck: the open door, the two women
side by side on the sofa

in their black headscarves,
mother and daughter perhaps,

unmoving, unspeaking, a loaf of bread
on the table, a cat asleep on the armchair.

Look away and it's sun on the wavetops, cicadas,
swallows shuttling on blue. Look back . . .

I almost had it, almost had it in one,
then the mother got up and closed the door.

BLOCKED

Clouds on the face of the mountain, stones on the ground,
birds in the air. He walks a little way,
then turns back. The valley's a bed of thistles. In the window
of the only house, a blue jug. Who is to blame for all this?
The poem shrugs him off.
Words are defined by what they dare not say.

XIX TRISTICHS

I flipped my cigarette-butt out of the window
into the cistern. Is it still glowing
or is that a shooting star?

*

He climbed the tower to toll the bell.
A bird looked him straight in the eye.
He sat down, then, and lit a cigarette.

*

The roses on your piano
shed a petal with each note you play.
Is that my fault? Is it?

*

Your sleep – a quiet lake.
A deer stoops to drink. I stoop
to drink.

*

What if these stones
fall into the sea? What if someone builds
a stone monument at the sea's edge?

*

When the shadow of a bird
falls on the white wall opposite,
I'll write you that letter.

*

She upturned the coffee cup.
'I see a door into the future.'
Open or closed? She didn't say.

*

The windows shuttered, the house empty
apart from the sleek and naked
absence of your body on the bed.

*

Those starlit nights . . . You could hear the apples
falling into the damp grass.
We let the apples lie, but gathered up the sound.

*

White light of noon.
White marble statues.
That white bird knows my mind.

*

A wind off the mountain
fills the bedrooms:
fir-trees, pines, cypresses, an eagle.

*

A fish wrapped in paper.
When it leaped for the light
glass in the windows glittered.

*

The hare knows your footstep;
she knows your fear
better than you yourself.

*

Rose-pearl light of dawn. Three boats,
barely visible. Flowers in one; in another,
oranges; in the third, my mother.

*

A word spoken in morning light
is a different word
in the light of evening.

*

Now he knows your secret
he will keep it always
on the very tip of his tongue.

*

The spider spins
a gallows-tree
of lace for the lacewing.

*

Noon. The clang
of the blacksmith's hammer.
This moment's mine.

*

I'll rise at dawn.
I'll put on a white shirt.
I'll be there before you wake.

DOUBLE

There are two of him, one inside the other.
How could you ever know

since the hidden one
is too clever to speak? But watch

closely as he eats
a late dinner by lamplight,

you'll see him lift the fork
to his mouth slowly,

steadily, as a mother does
when feeding her child.

Her greedy, growing child.

FEVERISH

Small squares on the move, merging, pulling apart,
building bricks unbuilding, a city of windows inside
a city of windows, everything hanging
on two right-angles, free-standing, out of whack
but somehow holding, somehow safe you decide
at the very moment they crack and start
to collapse (in utter silence) all of a heap
where three fleabitten dogs set off at an easy lope
going first through one small square
then another, and etcetera, the scent of the alien dead
ripe in their nostrils . . . and now they head
for the far end, as far back, as far down as you dare,
where a naked woman holds up
to the looking-glass, still weeping, a skinless hare.

from THE BRIDGE

I know that's his telephone ringing
in a far room. I also know

he's dead and I think I know
why the phone is ringing. I know it's none

of my business, but I somehow feel
if I picked up the call

everything would make sense. I know
I don't have what it takes

to break down his door, but there it is,
on his bedside table, next to a glass half-full

of water and (of course) his ashtray – the phone:
a tiny, uncrossable bridge

to days that never dawned
in that unremembered autumn. And so,

yes, it's just as if I'd taken the call, but I know
I could never own up to that.

GRAVITY

Full moon on the windowpane, a stamp
on an undelivered letter.

The furniture shop is shut. It's just
chairs and tables, mirrors, the usual stuff.

A dog stands four-square in the avenue of lights
and barks at its own shadow. You can throw

what you like at the moon, it's sure to fall
into the shadow of itself

like a coin tossed on a wager
coming down tails, and all the worse for you.

NIGHT-WIND

On the table, a glass half-full of water, a comb, a paper-knife,
a cigarette still burning in the ashtray.
Out in the courtyard a brace of duck, their feathers
ruffled by the night-wind. Such melancholy.

from HINTS

That ancient coin in your pocket: had you forgotten?
Your finger traces the young god's nakedness.

*

A man standing in darkness smiles a secret smile.
Is that because he can see in the dark? Maybe; or maybe
because he can see the dark.

*

The sunflowers almost hide the wall, the wall
hides the road completely. Beyond that you've got houses,
trees, hills, certain wrongdoings . . . In the heat of the day,
men from the lumber-yard go down to take a piss.
At night the dead come out to whitewash the wall.

*

Want to know what's truly important (he asked) about art?
I'll tell you. It's everything you leave out, whether or not
you mean to: like that knife in the basket there, hidden
under the grapes. Under the purple grapes.

*

No gift of words all year. Even so, his lamp
burns all night
in case a poem should stumble in.

*

He walked away from the market-place, the babble,
the second-hand fridges, the bowls and baskets,
'fresh produce' on the turn or else gone over.
He went into his house, he closed his door, he sat in his chair,
he sharpened his pencil (slowly, carefully) and wept.

*

Given a last request, they asked
for a paper-bag apiece which, somehow, someone found,
whereupon they blew them up and, turning, burst
the bags against the wall, then dropped like stones.

THE KISS

The sea was dark in the sun. He put his mouth on hers.
How strange, that coming together.
Her spittle was wine and salt. Later he took salt
from the tip of her breast with the tip of his tongue.

She woke to a scream and went to the window.
There were cats on the ridge-tiles. An old woman
was reading a letter by the glow from a streetlamp.
Music ran under the sound of the sea.

Next morning, they walked through an avenue of statues:
broken limbs, blind eyes taking the light.
'I have never loved anyone,' he said. 'Surely you know that.'
The scent of trodden herbs was everywhere.

THE ENVELOPE

He walks in the rain – no hurry . . .

The railings glisten; the trees
are black, with a faint red underblush;
there's an old bus-tyre in the sheep-pen.

The blue house looks much bluer in this light.

It's all a means to make nothing
less than it was. Rockfall. A clenched fist.
In the river, an empty envelope; perhaps
your name and address are on the other side.

LOPSIDED

He chalked a lopsided square on the floor.
He drew a door and stepped inside. He drew
a window; then, in a corner, the outline of a woman.

Light from the window struck
a glitter off the crystal chandelier.
The woman was naked: she would have to be.

It wasn't a question of belief,
we all knew that. After a moment he stepped
back through the door and shrugged
and brushed the chalk-dust from his hands.

LOSING HAND

The flowers were dying in their vases. A fly
blattered at the window.

'I'll have to go,' she said, 'I've had enough…this wind…'
He threw down his cards.

Just then, they heard a step on the stair. The door
opened a fraction, shedding a line of light.

They waited. No one. The deep, dark scent
of the flowers, the maddened fly . . .

She got down on her knees
to pick up the cards from the floor,

and handed them back, as someone might
who had just returned after many years away.

MORNING

She threw back the shutters and spread
the bedsheets on the window-sill.

It was broad day. A bird stared back at her.
'I'm alone, I'm alive . . .' She stood in front of the mirror.

'This, too, is a window. If I jump,
I'll fall into my own arms.'

PENELOPE

Not that she was fooled by his disguise:
she'd have known him by his scars for sure,
by the way he cast his eye
over the dead and dying suitors.

What was there to say? Twenty years of waking dreams,
now here he stood in the fire's last light,
a greybeard dappled with gore. 'Welcome,' she said,
in a voice she barely knew, he barely recognised.

Her loom cast latticed shadows on the ceiling.
The grave-cloth she'd worked to destroy
hung on the frame like something flayed.
Shapes in the weave darkened to ash
and lifted off, black birds of night
low on the skyline and disappearing fast.

SUDDENLY

A quiet night, so quiet, so still, and you
have stopped waiting. Then, somehow,
his touch on your face, electric, as if—

He'll come. Though all at once
a wind is getting up, the shutters are banging,
and the sound of the sea is a distant, drowning voice.

from PHILOCTETES

When they cook for us they cook
also for the dead. They take
our honey and oil from the table

and carry them to the catacombs.
If one of us knocks his plate with his spoon,
the rest of us turn as if to a tap on the shoulder.

Are these urns for ashes or jugs for wine?
Who can tell
what is ours and what belongs to the dead?

XX TRISTICHS

A hallway of doors. A grandfather clock.
The woman came out naked, her hair wrapped in a towel.
She didn't look at the clock. It wasn't that.

*

An insect on the window-pane, a burnt
match by the bedroom door:
something, or nothing at all?

*

I will bring this poem to an end
with an eyelash on your cheek
or a butterfly snarled in your hair.

*

It's hot. Clothes dry on balconies.
And, yes, here's the old woman in black.
The sun blanks her glasses.

*

Stone angels among broken columns
exchange kisses
over the graves of the long-since dead.

*

You passed me a glass of water
into which you had secretly
dipped your finger.

*

A train passing a village
late one Saturday. Indigo smoke.
A lone traveller.

*

They fed him honey, wine and cheese. They took him
to the arcades. In the hall of mirrors he saw
the young god, naked, his boots laced with gold.

*

Look – the new moon has just
slipped
a knife into her sleeve.

*

Pi-dogs. Dusty trees. A broken
balcony. A door into the night.
I have set my foot on the stairway.

*

She drops her bouquet on the bed.
She combs out her hair.
She strips off and goes to the window.

*

Each night, as you close your eyes, the unnameable
stands naked by your bed. It gazes
down at you and tells you everything.

*

With mother gone he makes his own coffee, he makes
his own bed. He's doing fine. His hands
have grown large, like mother's.

*

The sun finally reaches the backroom window.
Someone shouts outside in the street.
These things seem different to the loveless.

*

Black this side and white the other.
Your task – to make it
white this side and black the other.

*

Leaves step lightly on the nightwind;
in my sleep I hear them
and follow right down to the taproot.

*

Imagine the restaurant, halogen-bright, the clash
of voices, the clash of dishes. Then silence as she
removes her shoes. As she begins to dance.

*

A closed house. A staircase.
A goldfish swims
in the tarnished mirror.

*

Your dress still pegged on the line.
A breeze fills it.
Suddenly, evening's here.

*

The entire city reflected
in your emerald ring:
my little house on the outskirts.

THE MIRROR

He stood four-square to the mirror
and stared, unblinking, until he couldn't see
who it was, any more than he could recognise
the man who stood at his shoulder,
or that other man walking in, or the rest
crowding the glass, their faces
crumpled as if the silvering had slipped.

THE SHIRTS

'You know, I suppose, that death is nothing more
than an ugly rumour,' he said.
'There's nothing on earth to show that death exists.'

'I know it as only the dead can,' she replied.
'You'll find your shirts in the top drawer, neatly ironed.
All I lack is a rosebud or – if you can – a rose.'

THE WAX MUSEUM

In that dim light the naked, painted dummies
delivered a soft erotic charge. Their bodies
were perfect, as if they'd come
from a single mould, but when he looked more closely
he seemed to see his face among their faces.

There were footsteps in the hallway. He stripped off
and took his place, stone-still, with all the others
as the visitors toured the room. A woman said,
'They made a botch of this one,' then she laughed.
His eyelashes rustled as he closed his eyes.

THREE-STOREY HOUSE WITH BASEMENT

Top floor: eight students, penniless.
First floor: five milliners, two dogs.
Ground floor: the landlord and his 'daughter'.
Basement: the lumber and the rats.

The rat-run goes to the roof by way of the chimney.
From up there, at night, you get a perfect view
of blackberry clouds, of gardens, the lights of cafés.

A train goes by; its after-shock
sings in the brickwork. One of the first-floor women
gets up, her mouth full of pins, and slams the shutter.

THROUGH THE WINDOW

Bones and rusted iron. A goodwife pulling greens,
legs bare to her backside. The child left under a tree

with a dog standing guard. When night came on
we walked into town and happened to glance

through an open window. There they were,
man and wife, eating by lamplight. You could tell

everything from the way they dipped their heads,
unspeaking, and spooned their food.

Another man was standing at the table,
peeling an apple: slow turn of the knife. He said,

'Things never change for the likes of us,' by which
he might have meant sin or forgetfulness or loss.

DON'T ASK

It might be a nightclub logo
laying highlights on the pavement after rain,
or the sound of a cistern spilling,

or the silky splash
of a raindrop striking a rose, or you might decide
on the dark-out-of-darkness sob of a nightingale . . .

I glanced across and noticed how she slept
with her knee tucked up
and knew what I felt wasn't love, although, somehow,

the moment held all there was of tenderness:
the smell of the sheet, the fold of her knee, the fold
of the coverlet, that this was a warm evening in spring.

Look, who can say what these things mean?
They make patterns in our lives and all I know
is not knowing helps, but I couldn't tell you why.

THE CURE

Although the fever had left him months before,
he kept to his bed: the room a swelter of sweat and booze,
that meaty smell from the hide draped on the floor.

The creature had been skinned alive, he said;
the underside of the pelt still carried the pain
and sometimes, at night, you could see its hackles rise.

Once he dreamed that he got out of bed
and stood astride the thing. It made a back
to carry him out of his sick-room into the hall,
then breakneck through the kitchen, through the yard,
and down the street to the sound of whistles and drums.

ARCHAEOLOGY

This would be the agora: you can see where houses stood
at the perimeter. The theatre was set in the hillside. Now it's just stones
and thorn-bushes and lizards.
                              Midday summer heat, cicadas . . .
A shepherd shouts down the dry well. His echo comes back
to shroud him. When he turns, his dog backs off and bares its teeth.

On a white wall, the shadow of a naked man on horseback.

THE SAME STAR

Moonlight drenches the rooftops. The women pull their shawls
round tight and rush indoors to hide their tears.

He thinks there must be a woman in every mirror, naked, locked in.
He thinks the woman he's thinking of fell asleep

smelling the faint odour of a distant star,
the self-same whiff of scorch that now keeps him awake.

THE LEAST OF IT

'No, I'm fine,' he said, 'it's quiet the way I like it.'

The windows in the old people's home stay shut
right through the autumn months.

There used to be a horse tethered to that tree;
the rope's still there, lying slackly in the dust.

EVIDENCE

She was on the bed where he'd left her.
He took out his glass eye and put it on the bedside table.
'Now do you believe me?' he said, then turned as if to go.
She held the eye between finger and thumb to watch him.

THE ONE-ARMED MAN

Rain on the picture windows; rain-light grey as ash; along the hall
four circular tables, evenly spaced. The one-armed man
stood by the second table. Was he angry? Perhaps. Anyway,
we could see he'd have nothing to do with any of it.
His arm was red to the wrist. He carried a small notebook.
What would happen next was anybody's guess.

from HELEN

The air in the house is made heavy by the presence of the dead.
A trunk opens with no one near it. Dresses topple out
and shuffle upright; they walk the corridors. Curtains are drawn
by the ever-present no one. A cigarette burns in the ashtray,
left there by a man who just stepped out for a moment.
He's in the far room, standing close to the wall to hide his face.

[...]

Why do the dead stay here? No one wants them.
Why have they got themselves up in their Sunday best,
their carefully polished shoes never quite touching the floor?
Why do they act as if they owned the place, taking the fireside chairs,
leaving taps in the bathroom running, leaving soap
to dissolve in the tub? The servants go among them with brooms
and dusters and never notice a thing, except now and then a maid
will laugh and her laughter is caught and held like a tethered bird.

[...]

There came a day when I was feeling better. I asked the serving girls
to put my make-up on for me, which they did,
then brought me a mirror. My face was green, my lips black.
'Thank you,' I said, 'thank you, it makes all the difference.'
One of them got into my costume from the old days
then jumped up on the table and started to dance in my style.
She wasn't pretty. She had fat legs. From where I sat
I could see, high on her thigh, the yellowing bruise of a love-bite.

ON THE SUBJECT OF COLOUR

No colours, he said – none . . . except, perhaps,
browns and greys and near-whites – ash-tones, sombre and tested.
But his open mouth showed red, and a lilac shadow lay on his underlip.

THE POTTER

His staple was pitchers and pots, so who knows why,
when he'd finished his quota one time, he made a woman
with some left-over clay? Her breasts were full and firm.

When he got home his wife asked what had kept him;
she asked him several times, but got no answer;
the potter was lost in thought.
                              Next day, he made sure
there was clay enough for another woman
much like the first, and the next day, and the next.
He never went home. His wife packed up and left.

Now each morning he sings as he works,
naked among the clay women,
their sealed mouths, blind eyes, deaf ears, their bitten breasts.

TRAPPED

In the house across the street, in a room
directly opposite his, was a long mirror. When he looked

out of his window, he would see himself in the room
like a thief caught in a trap. He threw a stone.

His neighbour ran in to the sound of breaking glass,
then came to the window and shouted across:

'Thank God for that: whenever I looked in my mirror
there you were, doing something shifty behind my back.'

The first man turned away. The long mirror in his room
brought him face to face with his neighbour, knife in hand.

REVERSALS

There are graves under the houses and houses
under the graves and linking the three

a broad stone staircase where the dead
go up and the living go down. They pass one another

wordlessly which might mean they don't know, or else
they're pretending not to know. You can smell

the orange grove on the hill; you can hear
children bowling barrel-hoops down the street.

Two women gossip as they fill their jug at the spring.
Their secrets cloud the water.

Later they walk back through an avenue
of cypresses, carrying the jug like a bastard child.

THAT NIGHT

As soon as he switched on the light he knew who he was
and where he was: himself, here in his own room, safe
from the long reach of the night. To be sure of it
he stood in front of the mirror. But what to make
of those keys on the greasy string around his neck?

RAIN

Music drifts in from somewhere . . . is that why
he starts to cry for no good reason, or is it because
he's getting old? They came to fix the roof
but still the rain gets through, soaking his clothes,
his books, his manuscripts.
                                          The blind fiddle-player
stands out in the rain on Platform One
as the trains barrel through. His notes
are raindrops, or else the raindrops are notes.

THE BLACK BOAT

You think you can second-guess your life
by reading the stars. What can I tell you? Tonight
things are as they are; tomorrow, who knows?

The moon throws a skitter-skim of light
on the waves, enough for you to see
the black boat coming in, that shadowy figure at the oars.

THE LAST SUMMER

Soft shades of evening fade . . . Now we must start
to pack up: books, manuscripts, clothes.
Don't forget that pink dress, it really suits you,
although, of course, it will hang in the closet all winter.

I've been re-working the poems I wrote
over the last few months, but to tell the truth
they seem pretty thin to me now;
I can see through them to where one dark thought
lies between the lines, that this summer –
cicadas, pines, the sea, the ships, the sunsets,
skiffs riding the swell under balconies in the moonlight –
this summer, its soft, false words and smiles, will be my last.

Yannis Ritsos's short lyric poems are built on intensity and mood. Often, they provide a brief, compressed narrative that is hard-focused on specifics: weather, domestic paraphernalia, colour, time of day. Description is unfailingly evocative and (or because) reliant on close observation. They are spare, though not scant; they possess – and project – an emotional resonance that is instinctively subversive.

A few years back, I published a sequence of poems (*Marriage*) very loosely based on the relationship between Pierre Bonnard and his lover, model and life-long companion Marthe de Meligny. The poems traded off the twin notions of scrutiny – the fierceness of the painter's fix on his model – and something I called 'the mysteries of domesticity': those unsayable hints and harmonies, rituals and secrecies, that lie beneath the surface of any long relationship. I think I must have had Ritsos in mind when I developed that theory. His work is rooted in the quotidian but is, at the same time, freighted with mystery:

> Our women are distant; their sheets smell of goodnight.
> They put bread on the table as a token of themselves.

Sometimes the poems are invested with the fractured logic of dream, with dream-like images and events, or are set in a dream-scape that grows, as you read further, increasingly recognisable, no less strange, always compelling. At the same time, his locations and references are redolent of a wholly recognisable Greece: the balconies, the geraniums, statuary, the women in their blacks, and, enduringly, the sea. His touch is light, but his effect is profound. Much depends on image provoking narrative movement. The poems are so pared-down, so distilled, that the story-fragments we are given – the tiny psychodramas – have an irresistible potency. 'The more I take away the bigger it gets', said Alberto Giacometti and the same powerful reticence is a characteristic of Ritsos's shorter poems.

There's a real sense in which these loaded lyrics tend to resist the critical mill. This tristich is an example:

The sun finally reaches the backroom window.
Someone shouts outside in the street.
These things seem different to the loveless.

The notion of disorientation (akin, perhaps, to the effect of a mild virus) when heightened emotion sets us at odds with the world, when scents turn sour, when a view of the garden grows bleak, when household objects shed their purpose, is perfectly evoked in those three lines. There's immediate recognition of a precarious ontological state linked to a history until, a moment later, we realise that we can see that street, see that window. See *through* that window.

To say that Ritsos was prolific is to seriously understate the case. In his lifetime he published well in excess of 100 books, most often collections of poetry, though some fiction, translations and literary criticism. His *oeuvre* is in excess of 5,000 pages. In each of three separate years – 1972, 1974 and 1975 – he published seven collections of poems; in 1978 he published eleven. Of the 135 poems in *Doorbell* (1976), 126 were written in fewer than three weeks. If this output seems close to superhuman, it's worth remembering that it was achieved in the face of persistent ill-health, personal tragedy, and persecution first by the Metaxas regime, when his books were burned, next during the Greek Civil War, when his allegiance to Communism led to internment, and then by the Papadopoulos military dictatorship when he was again imprisoned, almost certainly tortured, and subsequently sent to island prison camps. During his time in the camps he continued to write even though writing was a proscribed activity. He would put the poems into tin cans and bury them around the compound to preserve them.

I first encountered Ritsos's poems in versions by Alan Page, published in 1969 as a pamphlet by Ian Hamilton's little magazine, *the Review*. I was immediately drawn to them. In the years that followed, I made a few versions of my own. Though this never constituted any sort of project, I often went back to his work and was always taken up by its wholly idiosyncratic compression and power: the way the poems have a tendency to detonate at the touch. When, finally, I found myself working on a coherent version of Ritsos it was, I think, because I wanted to tap in to that. I felt there was something in it for me – a way of getting inside those dark lines to take their scent and flavour.

Ritsos's compositional tendency vacillated between short lyrics and much longer poems: dramatic monologues, extended narratives, and what the poet himself referred to as 'choral poems': poems for voices. They are ambitious, confidently sustained and complex in the way they conflate autobiography, myth, allegory, codified political comment and systematic anachronism. There are, though, in these extended pieces, passages that stand out – almost advertise themselves – as close kin to the short poems. I gave in, gladly, to an impulse to filch some of these passages and co-opt them to my purpose. The most radical example of this sort of reduction is my extreme condensation of a dramatic monologue, 'The Dead House'.

My method in selecting the poems for this volume was simple enough. I read as much of Ritsos's massive output as is available in translation and worked on the poems that spoke to me most strongly. Like other poets making versions of poems in a language of which they are either wholly ignorant, or in which they are far from fluent, I compared texts, using as many translations as were available to me, but also asked Greek speakers to provide me with sternly literal word-for-word translations by way of comparison, and then worked from all these sources. In some cases my versions more or less resemble the originals; in many what I have written might better be called an adaptation or *hommage*. And just as some poems have been adapted so, occasionally, have titles.

The arguments for free versions over close translations have been well-rehearsed. It's enough to say that the poem one is to render into English (and let's assume we're talking about a good poem) will have its essence in what is specifically untranslatable: in cadence, in colour, in nuance, in weight-of-word, in hint, in association, in tone, *in music*. A poet's vocabulary isn't dictionary-definable and translations that provide a literal summary of what the poet said – of narrative line, of description – are street-maps of the place, not the place itself. It is, of course, the very accuracy that defeats the intention. A version is an attempt to re-imagine the piece, to test its pulse, to make a new poem in English that delivers its truth while ignoring the apparent truth that lies in pre-cise representation. That transformation is what I have attempted here.

D.H.

May 2012

FRIENDS OF ENITHARMON

The following have generously become Patrons and Sponsors
of the *Friends of Enitharmon* scheme, enabling this
and other publications to come into being:

PATRONS

Duncan Forbes
Sean O'Connor
Masatsugu Ohtake
Myra Schneider

SPONSORS

Kathy & Jeff Allinson
Colin Beer
Natasha Curry
Vanessa Davis
Jack Herbert
Alison M. Houston
Sylvia Riley
Angela Sorkin
Janet Upward